Katie and the Dinosaurs

James Mayhew

ORCHARD BOOKS

*For Robert, Rebecca, Victoria
and my goddaughter Elizabeth*

If you would like to know how to say the
names of all the dinosaurs in the story, please
turn to the back of the book.

ORCHARD BOOKS
338 Euston Road, London NW1 3BH
Orchard Books Australia
Level 17/207 Kent Street, Sydney, NSW 2000
ISBN 978 1 84362 396 0
First published in Great Britain in 1991
First paperback publication in 1994
This edition published in 2004
Text and illustrations © James Mayhew 1991
The right of James Mayhew to be identified as the author and
illustrator of this work has been asserted by him in accordance
with the Copyright, Designs and Patents Act, 1988.
A CIP catalogue record for this book is available from
the British Library.
5 7 9 10 8 6 4
Printed in China
Orchard Books is a division of Hachette Children's Books,
an Hachette Livre UK company.
www.hachettelivre.co.uk

"Come and look, Grandma, come and see the dinosaurs!" said Katie.

Katie loved the natural history museum, and she wanted to show her Grandma everything.

"They're just a load of old bones," said Grandma.

"Well, you're really old," said Katie. "There must have been dinosaurs alive when you were little."

"I'm not that old!" snorted Grandma, looking for somewhere to sit down. They found a seat next to a skeleton of a very fierce looking dinosaur.

"Why don't you go and look at your horrible dinosaurs while I have forty winks," said Grandma.

"They're not horrible," sniffed Katie. "But I do wish they weren't just skeletons." And she skipped off on her own, taking her picnic lunch with her, just in case she got hungry.

Katie saw spiky dinosaurs, fishy dinosaurs, flying dinosaurs, horned dinosaurs, long dinosaurs....

She closed her eyes and tried to imagine they were alive. She thought they must have been very frightening with their sharp teeth and claws.

Next to one of the dinosaurs was a corridor. Katie set off down it to make sure she hadn't missed anything worth seeing.

The corridor was long and dark, and there was no one in sight. Katie began to feel scared. She looked for a *Way Out* sign, but there didn't seem to be one. She was lost.

"Now what do I do?" said Katie crossly.

She came to a big door with a notice on it that said:

ABSOLUTELY NO ADMITTANCE WHATSOEVER

"I'll just take a quick look," said Katie and she opened the door and stepped through.

The door led outside and there in front of her was a dinosaur!
It was no bigger than Katie, but it was a real live one!

"Hello," said Katie. "Who are you?"

"Hadrosaurus," said the dinosaur. "Who are *you*?"

"I'm Katie," said Katie, "and I think I'm lost."

"I'm lost too," said Hadrosaurus. "I was chased by a
Tyrannosaurus Rex."

"Isn't that the really fierce dinosaur?" asked Katie.

"That's right," said Hadrosaurus. "Now I don't know how to get home."

"Don't worry," said Katie. "I'll be able to see where we are from the top of this hill," and she clambered up a steep slope.

"This isn't a hill!" said Hadrosaurus, scrambling up behind her.

Katie gasped. "Oh, it's a Brontosaurus!"
She was very high up and she could see for miles.

"Now show me where you live," said Katie.

"I think it's somewhere over there, along the river bank," said Hadrosaurus.

Katie looked across the river.

"What are those funny-looking birds?" she asked.

"They're Pterosaurs," said Hadrosaurus. "Watch out!"

But one of the Pterosaurs had already spotted Katie's yellow scarf. It swooped towards her and before Katie could duck, it had snatched the scarf from her.

"Hey, that's mine! Bring it back!" yelled Katie.

But the Pterosaur was far away already.

Now the Brontosaurus started to move. She was getting fed up with those two noisy creatures jumping about on her back. How they made her itch!

Katie hung on for dear life, slipping and sliding about on the Brontosaurus's back as she lumbered down to the river for a nice cool bathe. She was so huge that Katie and Hadrosaurus hardly got wet at all.

From high up on the Brontosaurus's back Katie could look right out to sea. All sorts of strange creatures were swimming there. She recognized some of them from the museum – the Ichthyosaurs with their long snouts, and a Plesiosaur with its snakelike neck.

Before long the Brontosaurus reached the edge of the water.

"Let's go," said Katie. Followed by Hadrosaurus, she slid all the way down to the tip of the Brontosaurus's tail and they landed in a giggling heap on the ground.

The Brontosaurus chuckled a deep thundery laugh.

"Which way now?" said Katie.

"Into the jungle," said Hadrosaurus.

The jungle was hot and sticky. Through the trees Katie could see a herd of enormous dinosaurs.

"What on earth are those?" asked Katie. "I don't like the look of *them*."

"Only Stegosaurs," said Hadrosaurus. "They won't hurt us."

"Are you sure?" said Katie suspiciously, as one Stegosaur licked its lips.

"Oh yes, they only eat plants," said Hadrosaurus. So Katie gave them some grass. Then they went on through the jungle and soon the trees began to thin out.

Suddenly Hadrosaurus let out a squeal! "Mama! Papa!" he shouted.

It was Hadrosaurus's family.

His Mama and Papa hugged him and hugged Katie too for bringing him home.

"I hope you're not going to eat me," worried Katie.

"Don't be afraid, Katie," said Hadrosaurus, "we only eat plants too."

That reminded Katie that she hadn't had her picnic lunch yet.

She was feeling quite hungry by now, but she politely shared her cucumber sandwiches and chocolate biscuits. She saved her meat pie for later.

Plant-eating dinosaurs from far and wide picked up the smell of Katie's sandwiches, and padded across the rocks towards her.

There was a Styracosaurus and a Triceratops with their horns,
an Iguanodon with his spiky thumbs and some Ankylosaurs.
    The dinosaurs shook some strange-looking fruits out of
the trees and they all ate until they were full.
    It was the best picnic Katie had ever had.

Suddenly, another dinosaur crashed out of the jungle. It was Tyrannosaurus Rex! He had been following Katie and Hadrosaurus all along.

He grunted and growled and ground his teeth, and swished his tail and stamped his scaly feet. He was hungry! And he didn't want cucumber sandwiches or chocolate biscuits, he wanted meat! He wanted Katie!

"Quick, run for your life!" said the Hadrosaurs, and Katie took to her heels.

All the dinosaurs ran away in alarm.

Tyrannosaurus Rex thundered after Katie and the dinosaurs as
they ran through the jungle towards the river.
Katie got out of breath, but she kept on running.

At last she could see the museum ahead of her. If only she had
stayed safely inside!

Then she remembered the meat pie. She tore open her lunch
box and threw a piece at the Tyrannosaurus Rex.

The Tyrannosaurus stopped in his tracks. He sniffed the piece of pie. He ate it up. He liked it so much that Katie threw him the rest, even though she had been saving it for herself. And the Tyrannosaurus Rex padded off into the jungle again, contentedly clutching Katie's lunch box.

"Whew! That was close!" said Katie.

It was getting late now so Katie turned to say goodbye to Hadrosaurus.

"I do wish you could come home with me," she said, "but Grandma would only scream and make a fuss."

"I'm happy here with my family anyway," said Hadrosaurus. He gave Katie a lick. "Thank you for helping me find them."

"BLEAGH!" spluttered Katie, as dinosaurs have very sloppy tongues. Then she went back through the door into the museum.

This time Katie easily found her way through the museum.
Grandma was waiting where she had left her.

"Where on earth have you been?" asked Grandma.

"I've seen all kinds of dinosaurs," said Katie. "Why don't you
come and have a look too?"

"All right," said Grandma. "Where do we start?"

"This way," said Katie, and, taking her hand, off they went.

More about Katie's dinosaurs

Dinosaurs ('terrible lizards') lived many millions of years ago and all died out very suddenly. Nobody knows why this happened.

We can still find out a lot by looking at their bones. These bones are called fossils because they have been trapped and preserved in rock. We can tell how long ago the dinosaurs lived, what they ate, and best of all, what they looked like.

Perhaps there is a museum near you where you can see dinosaur bones or even whole skeletons. Remember how very old they are, and try to imagine, as Katie did, what they must have looked like.

Here is the meaning of the names of all the dinosaurs in the story and how to say them:

Hadrosaurus – big lizard
(HAD-row-SAW-rus)

Tyrannosaurus Rex – king of tyrant lizards
(Tie-RAN-oh-SAW-rus Rex)

Stegosaur – plated lizard
(STEG-oh-saw)

Triceratops – three-horned face
(Try-SERRA-tops)

Styracosaurus – spiky lizard
(Sty-RACK-oh-SAW-rus)

Ichthyosaur – fish lizard
(IK-thee-oh-saw)

Plesiosaur – near-to-lizard
(PLESS-ee-oh-saw)

Pterosaur – flying lizard
(TEH-row-saw)

Brontosaurus – thunder lizard
(BRON-tow-SAW-rus)

Iguanodon – iguana tooth
(Ig-you-ARN-a-don)

Ankylosaur – rounded lizard
(An-KILL-oh-saw)